WHAT IS ART?

Paintings

KAREN HOSACK

CHICAGO, ILLINOIS

Editorial: Adam Miller, Charlotte Guillain, Clare Lewis,
and Catherine Veitch
Design: Victoria Bevan and AMR Design Ltd
Illustrations: David Woodroffe
Picture Research: Mica Brancic
and Helen Reilly/Arnos Design Ltd
Production: Victoria Fitzgerald

Originated by Modern Age
Printed and bound by CTPS (China Translation and
Printing Services Ltd)

13 12 11 10 09
10 9 8 7 6 5 4 3 2 1

Library of Congress Cataloging-in-Publication Data
Hosack, Karen.
  Paintings / Karen Hosack.
    p. cm. -- (What is art?)
  Includes bibliographical references and index.
  ISBN 978-1-4109-3162-7 (hc)
  1. Painting--Juvenile literature. I. Title.
  ND1146.H67 2008
  750--dc22
                                    2008009696

Acknowledgments
The publishers would like to thank the following for
permission to reproduce photographs: Ashmolean
Museum p. **6**; © 2008 Banco de Mexico Diego Rivera
& Frieda Kahlo Museums Trust. p. **14** (Av. Cinco de
Mayo No.2, Col. Centro, Del. Cuauhtemoc 06059,
Mexico, D.F. Kahlo/University of Texas/Harry Ransom
Center); Corbis pp. **4** (Kazuyoshi Nomachi), **9** (Geoffrey
Clements), **10** (by kind permission of the Trustees of
the National Gallery, London), **18** (The Andy Warhol
Foundation for the Visual Arts); ©Robert Bechtle p. **23**
(© Copyright 64 Valiant. 1971/Art Resource, NY/Yale
University Art Gallery/Gift of Richard Brown Baker, B.A.
1935. 1982); © The Bridgeman Art Gallery pp. **5** & **12**
(Private Collection/© Christie's Images), **7**, **24** & **27**
(©ADAGP, Paris and DACS, London 2008), **8** (Private
Collection), **13** & **17** (National Gallery Collection),
15 (Musee d'Orsay, Paris, France, Giraudon), **16** (©
Succession Picasso/DACS 2008), **20** (©The Estate of
Roy Lichtenstein/DACS 2008), **21** (© ARS, NY and
DACS, London 2008), **22** (Longhi Collection, Florence,
Italy), **26** (Rijksmuseum, Amsterdam, The Netherlands);
© The Phillips Collection p. **25** (© ADAGP, Paris and
DACS, London 2008); © The Tate Gallery p. **19** (©
Chris Ofili, to Woman No Cry, 1998).

Cover picture of Olive Trees by Vincent van Gogh,
reproduced with permission of © Corbis.

Every effort has been made to contact copyright
holders of any material reproduced in this book.
Any omissions will be rectified in subsequent
printings if notice is given to the publishers.

Disclaimer
All the Internet addresses (URLs) given in this book
were valid at time of going to press. However, due
to the dynamic nature of the Internet, some addresses
may have changed, or sites may have changed or
ceased to exist since publication. While the author
and publishers regret any inconvenience this may
cause readers, no responsibility for any such changes
can be accepted by either the author or the publishers.
It is recommended that adults supervise children
on the Internet.

Contents

Any words appearing in the text in bold, **like this**,
are explained in the glossary.

What Is Painting?

At an art museum, you can see many different paintings. Some paintings are of things you see in real life, such as people, **landscapes**, and even soup cans. Other paintings are harder to understand.

Looking for clues

You do not need to know much about paintings to enjoy looking at them. By asking a few simple questions and exploring the answers, you can start to understand why and how people paint.

This painting is on a cave wall. The picture shows people hunting animals. Historians think people made these paintings to bring the hunters good luck.

Cave painting found in Algeria, from Cattle Period (4000–2000 BCE)

Waterliles by Claude Monet, 1908

Why paint?

People paint for many different reasons. Some artists paint to tell a story or give information. Claude Monet painted these waterlilies for a completely different reason. He belonged to a group of artists in the late 19th century. They wanted to show the beauty of nature in their paintings.

What Is Paint?

Paintings can be painted with anything that is wet. Traditionally, artists ground up colors they found in nature—for example, using flowers or rocks. They then mixed the powder with oil or egg yolk to make paint. People also mix these powders with water to make paints called **watercolors**. Modern paints are usually made from chemicals and mixed with a rubbery material.

The Hunt in the Forest by Paolo Uccello, c. 1460–65

Some natural paints were even made with beetles! Some beetles make a deep red or maroon pigment in their bodies. You can see how this looks in the painting above.

In this painting the artist has used very thick oil paint. If you could run your hand over the surface of the **canvas**, it would feel bumpy. It would have taken a long time to dry.

Composition No. 7 by Wassily Kandinsky, 1913

Thick or thin?

Today, you can buy oil paint in tubes. When you squeeze oil paint out of a tube, it is very thick. Artists can mix the oil paint with more oil to make it thinner, or use it as it is.

Did you know?
When artists use oil paint to give texture to a painting, it is called **impasto**.

Different Views of Nature

Here are two paintings by artists trying to show what they see in nature. Which one do you think looks more like real life? Both artists spent a long time in front of the **landscape** they painted. Can you tell what time of year it is in each painting? Where are the clues?

Autumn Trees by Egon Schiele, 1911

In this picture the leaves are red and orange. Some of them are falling off. What does this tell us about the season? Do you think the sky really looked like that, or has the artist added his own colors and textures?

Rocky Mountains by Albert Bierstadt, 1886

Getting deep

Would you want to go swimming in this lake? Or does it look too cold? The background is very misty. You can see through the mist to the mountains in the distance. This makes the painting seem deeper. This is called **perspective**. The leaves and branches on the trees make the front of the painting, or **foreground**, feel closer to us. The artist also uses color to do this.

Composing a Painting

The way all the parts of a painting are put together is called **composition**. Color is not the only way artists can change how a painting looks. There are other ways that painters help us to focus on the important part of a painting.

The Fighting Téméraire Tugged to Her Last Berth to Be Broken Up by J. M. W. Turner, 1838

This is a very famous painting of a ship called the *Téméraire*. The ship is being tugged up a river by a smaller steamboat to be broken up in a shipyard.

Getting focused

Look carefully at where the artist has put the main subject of the painting. If you measure an exact square from the right-hand edge of the painting, you will see that the mast of the *Téméraire* lies exactly on the left vertical. Also, if you draw a diagonal line from the top left-hand corner to the bottom right corner, you will notice that the tops of the masts also fall exactly on this line. This has all been carefully planned by the artist to make us naturally look at the focus of the painting.

Did you know?

The *Téméraire* helped to win an important battle between the French and the English, but when this painting was made it was no longer needed. The arrival of steam engines meant that its wind-powered sails were out of date.

A lot of thought and calculation goes into making a painting, although the end result can look natural and unplanned.

For Whom Was It Made?

Often artists make their paintings especially for somebody. If we know about the person a painting was made for, then we can try to understand why it was made.

Images of war

In 1918 the painter John Singer Sargent traveled to France to record British and U.S. soldiers during World War I. People at home had no other way of seeing what it was like for the soldiers.

Gassed by John Singer Sargent, 1918–19

This painting shows a group of soldiers who have been blinded by gas, waiting to see a doctor. What is the mood of the painting?

Did you know?
Before television was invented, people needed artists to show them what the war was like.

This painting was **commissioned** by the man on the left. Can you see the strange object on the floor? Can you guess what it is? Look at it from different angles.

The Ambassadors by Hans Holbein, 1533

The Ambassadors

You do not need to know who these two men are to guess what they like doing. Can you see the instruments on the top shelf? These are used to travel and **navigate**. They would have been the most up-to-date tools at the time. The items on the bottom shelf are all connected to **culture**, such as music and architecture.

Symbolism

Colors and objects in paintings can sometimes show feelings or ideas. This is called **symbolism**.

Painting pain

The painting below is a **self-portrait**. The artist had the disease polio at the age of six and was later in a vehicle accident. This meant she stayed in bed for a long time because she had many operations. Can you see how she is showing her own pain through her painting?

What do you think this artist is trying to say about herself? Look at her necklace. It is made of thorns and looks as though it is almost strangling her as it grows around her body.

Self-Portrait with Necklace of Thorns by Frida Kahlo, 1940

Model mother

This painting is a portrait of the artist's mother. Some people think there is symbolism about his relationship with his mother in the painting. He has painted the portrait from the side, so that we cannot see his mother's face very well. He has used very dark, cold colors. What do these things say about how he saw his mother?

Arrangement in Grey and Black No. 1: Portrait of the Artist's Mother by James McNeill Whistler, 1871

Perhaps the artist simply used his mother as a model and was not trying to show us how he felt about her at all. What do you think?

Think about it!
It is sometimes difficult to guess what an artist is trying to say in a painting. We have to be open to different people's ideas of what they think the meaning might be.

When Was It Made?

Paintings can tell us a lot about the time they were made. This painting by Pablo Picasso shows how terrible war can be. It is about the bombing of the Spanish city of Guernica in 1937. Picasso was Spanish, and he hated what the fighting was doing to his country. He includes a bull and a horse as symbols of Spain. An exploding light represents the bombs.

Guernica by Pablo Picasso, 1937

The twisted figures in this painting show the horror and confusion after the bombing.

Did you know?
This painting traveled to different countries shortly after it was finished. This was to raise awareness of the Spanish Civil War.

A bird has been placed in the flask and is slowly dying. What do the people around the table think about what is happening? Look at each of their expressions.

An Experiment on a Bird in the Air Pump by Joseph Wright, c. 1768

An experiment

This painting was made in the 18th century, at a time when people were very interested in science. The man at the center of the painting is a scientist. He would travel around to people's houses and entertain them with different experiments. Here he is creating a **vacuum** by taking all of the air out of the glass flask standing on top of a pump.

Repeating images

This **canvas** of soup cans also tells us something about the time in which it was made. Andy Warhol, the artist, created it using a process called screen printing. He could make many copies of the same image using this method. Warhol even called his studio the "Factory" because of the way he produced his work. He was a member of a group of artists known as the **Pop Art** movement.

One Hundred Campbell's Soup Cans by Andy Warhol, 1962

This repeated image of the same can was made at a time when factories were suddenly making large amounts of cheap products.

Did you know?

The name "Pop Art" comes from the word "popular." These artists' work and the things they painted were very popular with ordinary people.

No Woman, No Cry by Chris Ofili, 1998

No Woman, No Cry

This painting is by the British artist Chris Ofili. You can figure out
when and where the painting was made by looking at the woman's
tears. If you look carefully at the original, you can see a small collage
of a person in each tear. They all contain pictures of Stephen Lawrence,
a black teenager who was murdered in London in 1993. It is a sad
image with an important message.

A Bit of Style

Artists usually have their own style that they build over many years. Sometimes you can identify an artist by his or her style.

Pow! Bang! Splat!

The U.S. artist Roy Lichtenstein was interested in the way that comic strips tell a story. He used the same bold **primary colors** found in comics in his huge paintings. He tended to use close-up images to create a striking painting. Most famously, he used large words to show energy and action.

Reflections on Crash by Roy Lichtenstein, 1990

Lichtenstein used colored dots to make up his paintings. Images in comic books are also made this way.

Some people believe they can see figures moving in this painting, or perhaps the wildness of a storm in nature. What can you see?

Number 20 by Jackson Pollock, 1949

Drip drip

The U.S. artist Jackson Pollock was best known for making drip paintings like this one. He would place very large **canvases** or pieces of paper on the floor of his studio and throw and drip paint from different heights and angles at different speeds.

Almost Like a Photograph

The paintings of Caravaggio are known for looking very like real life. In this painting, a boy has placed his hand near the fruit on the table, but he had not seen the lizard hiding. Suddenly, its teeth snap around the child's finger. The boy's face shows pain and shock. His body tries to pull away from the danger. Caravaggio captures the moment as if it is a photograph, but cameras would not be invented for another 200 years.

Caravaggio managed to make his paintings look so real by studying very carefully how light bounces off people and objects. We call this contrast of light and dark in painting **chiaroscuro.**

Boy Bitten By a Lizard by Caravaggio, 1595–1600

Time standing still

Photorealists use cameras almost like sketchbooks. A photograph shows exactly what something looks like. But it is also a frozen moment in time. A photorealist tries to capture these moments on **canvas**. Things like the light, shadows, and the way the wind is blowing are all part of that second in time.

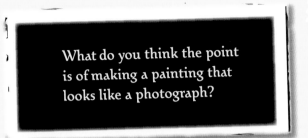

What do you think the point is of making a painting that looks like a photograph?

64 Valiant by Robert Bechtle, 1971

Say cheese

The U.S. artist Robert Bechtle used a camera when he produced this painting. He painted from the photograph. In fact, he has made a painting that looks almost exactly like a photograph. This style of painting is called **photorealism**. The painter's skill is in painting the glossiness of the image and the changes between the shadows and light.

I Had a Dream Like That!

At first glance, this painting by René Magritte looks like a nice view through a window. Look again and you will see that something strange is going on. Look at the artist's easel and the white dotted vertical line toward the center. This is the side of a **canvas**, and is in fact a painting within a painting. Magritte was a member of the **Surrealist** movement, which was a group of artists who were especially interested in painting dream-like images.

The Human Condition by René Magritte, 1935

Does this painting look like a dream to you?

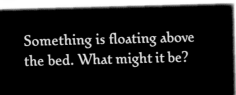

The Dream by Marc Chagall, 1939

Dream or nightmare?

Another artist who is well known for painting dream-like pictures is Marc Chagall. The title of this painting is *The Dream*. We can see a bed outside in a street with two figures sitting on it. What do you think they might be saying to each other? Perhaps one person is having the dream and the other one is trying to wake him or her up. Does it look like a nice dream or a nightmare to you? What else can you see?

What Can You See?

You do not need to know everything about a painting to start to understand it. Look carefully at what you can see and ask yourself lots of questions.

Look closely

You can tell lots of things about this woman from looking at this painting. You can tell from what she is wearing that she is fairly poor and that she lived a long time ago.

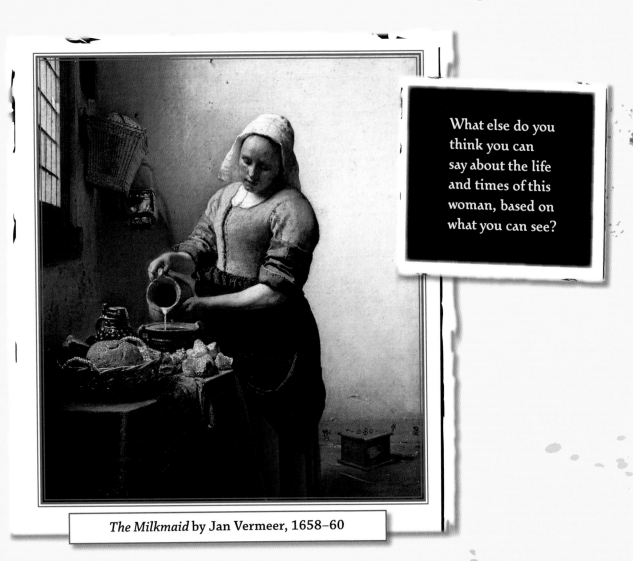

What else do you think you can say about the life and times of this woman, based on what you can see?

The Milkmaid by Jan Vermeer, 1658–60

This is another everyday scene. Again, just by looking at the picture, what can you tell about the men and the times they lived in? How are the people here different from the person in the painting on page 26?

The Constructors by Fernand Léger, 1950

Sharing paintings

We have seen how and why many artists make paintings. We have looked at different ways of using paint, the effect colors can have on the people looking at a painting, and how we can find clues in paintings that tell us more. In general, art is made by people for other people. It is a way of sharing important ideas with each other about our lives and our relationship with the world.

Timeline

Where to See Paintings

This map shows where some of the paintings in this book can be seen.

① Oxford, England
Ashmolean Museum: *The Hunt in the Forest*, Uccello

② London, England
The National Gallery:
  Boy Bitten by a Lizard, Caravaggio
  An Experiment on a Bird in the Air Pump, Joseph Wright of Derby
Tate Britain: *No Woman, No Cry*, Chris Ofili
Imperial War Museum:
  Gassed, John Singer Sargent

③ Amsterdam, The Netherlands
Stedelijk Museum:
  Reflections on Crash, Roy Lichtenstein
Rijksmuseum: *The Milkmaid*, Jan Vermeer

④ New York, New York
The Metropolitan Museum of Art: *Rocky Mountains*, Albert Bierstadt
Museum of Modern Art:
  Waterlilies, Claude Monet
Leo Castelli Gallery:
  One Hundred Campbell's Soup Cans, Andy Warhol

⑤ Paris, France
Musee d'Orsay:
  Arrangement in Grey and Black No. 1: Portrait of the Artist's Mother, James McNeill Whistler

⑥ Vienna, Austria
Osterreiche Galerie: *Autumn Trees*, Egon Schiele

⑦ Madrid, Spain
Reina Sofia National Museum Art Center:
  Guernica, Pablo Picasso

Glossary

canvas cloth material that many artists use to paint on

chiaroscuro contrast of light and dark in paintings

commission ask an artist to produce work for money

composition how a painting, drawing, or photograph is put together

culture customs of a particular time and group of people

foreground part of a picture that looks the closest

impasto thickly applied paint

kinesthetic art artwork that is created using movement and energy. The artist uses his or her whole body to create it.

landscape picture of outdoor scenery

navigate find the way to a destination

perspective technique that artists use to give pictures a feeling of space and distance

photorealism style of painting that looks like a photograph

Pop Art art movement in which artists used themes from popular culture in the 1950s and 1960s

primary colors colors that cannot be made by mixing other colors

self-portrait artist's picture of himself or herself

Surrealist 20th-century art movement that was interested in creating art that looked like a dream

symbolism using something that represents something else

canvas cloth material that many artists use to paint on

watercolor paint made from mixing colored pigments with water

Learn More

Books to read

Claybourne, Anna. *Body Painting (Body Art)*. Chicago: Heinemann Library, 2005.

Flux, Paul. *Color (How Artists Use)*. Chicago: Heinemann Library, 2008.

Spilsbury, Richard. *Pop Art (Art on the Wall)*. Chicago: Heinemann Library, 2008.

Thomson, Ruth. *What Is a Self-Portrait? (Art's Alive)*. Mankato, Minn.: Sea to Sea, 2005.

Websites to visit

All about surrealism, with examples of work
www.surrealism.org

All about the life and works of Picasso
www.artcyclopedia.com/artists/picasso_pablo

The Metropolitan Museum of Art's website for kids
www.metmuseum.org/explore/museumkids.htm

The National Gallery of Art's website for kids
www.nga.gov/kids/kids.htm

Index